Water's Edge

Michelle St. Romain Wilson
Alma Rosa Alvarez

Singing Bird Press
www.singingbirdpressashland.com

Water's Edge
Copyright 2023 by Michelle St. Romain Wilson
and Alma Rosa Alvarez

Published by Singing Bird Press

Cover photo: Michelle St. Romain Wilson
Back cover photo: Alma Rosa Alvarez

Library of Congress Control Number: 2023910047

ISBN: 979-8-218-21454-8

For all that is living. For all that gives life.

— Alma Rosa Alvarez

For my wife, Ellen, and our children - Evan, Reid, and Charlotte. You are the lights of my life. For my writing partners, past and present, whose love, friendship, and inspiration keep me going.

— Michelle St. Romain Wilson

Other Publications by Singing Bird Press

Promised Fruit, by Alma Rosa Alvarez and
Michelle St. Romain Wilson

Table of Contents

Introduction

These poems, written between 2020 and 2023, reflect life during a time of great upheaval and transformation in our world. A global pandemic, wildfires and hurricanes of epic proportions, and economic and political stresses all continue to play a part in the way our world is changing. And we must learn to change with it, to find not only resilience but also hope. Perhaps most importantly, we must find a common bond with all who are a part of our community.

We see our community as both local and global. We offer these pieces as reflections of our path: witnessing what is happening with clear eyes and an open heart; connecting with the living world around us; and healing through the power of connecting with our own creative and sacred spirits. We invite you to join us in this journey.

Michelle St. Romain Wilson (*MSW*) and
Alma Rosa Alvarez (*ARA*)

Witnessing

True Spectacle

Some landscapes
lack
human witnesses
meanwhile
the second growth trees
stand sentinel
to climate
to environment
while they sequester
carbon dioxide:
dozens of types of conifers
Douglas firs,
and over there--
an old pair of cedars

A short distance
and the ground is lined
with maidenhair,
sword ferns,
and the huckleberries,
sought out in spring and summer
by the Kalapuya people

Nearby
a freshwater spring
emerges

Young climate activists
engage in non-violent
camera-caught tactics
to block/ cutting
but the trees

and their habitat
if one takes
the time
to see
are the true spectacle.

ARA

Fruit Response

Warm October day
I beeline to figs
on a stand
surprised
there are still
some around

The farmer
touches the plumpness
under the purple skins
and then points
to the ones
ready this day
and the ones
that will be
ready tomorrow

Tenderly
she cradles
my purchase

These are her
first figs
since the fires

ARA

Elegy: Wind and Fire
Almeda Fire, Southern Oregon, September 2020

Move gently through this world
broken by fire and fear
racing through the veins of our bodies and this land

Tread lightly through the ash
which covers what remains:
       a child's broken tricycle
       cracked ceramic pots on burned doorsteps
       tables melted into unrecognizable shapes

Breathe slowly, intentionally
careful of the air thick with smoke
and particles of treasures once cherished
by our neighbors and friends

Walk through these roads with care
the lifelines of our valley
strewn now with charred debris
and phantom images
of houses and storefronts
foggy pictures of the mind
rising only in memory's eye
through the vacant air
above cement foundations
and cracked floors

The mountains stand guard in the distance
sentinels bearing witness
in silent reverie to our grief

Move with tenderness
toward every beating heart
in this beloved community
thick with grief and with memories
of all that was before

Breathe out with grace the gentle breeze of hope
for all that flickers in tender stages of gestation
for all that we must love
        into birth
        once again

MSW

Elegy: Wind and Water

Hurricane Laura, Lake Charles, Louisiana, August 2020

The water washed over my ancestors' graves
and I dreamed of angels, cloaked in green,
rising up from the sodden Earth
singing Allelujah in a tone
only the animals could hear:
the cows let free from the fields
because the time was too short to save them
from the coming hurricane
and the owls and squirrels and field mice
heard too, this song coming from
my ancestors' graves

The salt water blown into the Gulf
from Caribbean blue waters now pushed
its way onto the coastal shore
(which is washing away by
inches and feet each year)
and then up and through the rivers
and marshes and, finally, Lake Charles itself,
that body of water that held my own
when I swam there in summers
as a child
now brackish, it overflows
onto the banks of the city

The wind came before the water
as a trumpeter announcing the onset
of the storm
and people fled
or hid in boarded-up houses

or drank whiskey
until they could not
feel fear

And I watched from far away
as the newscasters came
from distant cities to stand
and show us all
what it is to be
in the eye of the hurricane
hoping for the eye of God
to watch over you

And still I heard my ancestors sing
though I wondered if anyone else could hear
with the drumbeat of the wind
and the crashing of the oak trees
their song a distant backdrop
to destruction of everything
their descendants built

I listened for the sounds of the crickets
for the whispers of the rabbits
or the almost silent flutter of the
butterfly wings stirring up the storm

Sixteen people lost their lives
when the water rose this time
but thousands more would have
had that eye not turned just slightly
to the East

following, perhaps, the eye of God
just enough to push
the walls of water
into the marshland around the city
washing over our ancestors' graves
saving the people who prayed for protection
from the un-survivable surge

The water must have heard
the ancestors singing
Allelujah
moving the tide with their whispers
toward the prayed-for
coming dawn

And their graves were blessed and baptized
and though the destruction was vast
the city did not flood
and people's lives were saved
and I hear our ancestors' voices
singing to us still

MSW

Canada Goose Nest

No matter
the prediction
from Punxsutawney Phil
of six more weeks
of winter
spring has intruded
into February

The Canada geese
have stopped mid-flight--
no longer going
to the Sacramento Valley

On the pastureland
down the hill
a female
has begun constructing
her nest
with pieces of this and that
and her own down
while the male
stands guard

All of us hold our breath
for the unpredictable
cold days that may come ahead
cold days
unkind to goslings
that won't know how to fly

ARA

The Counting Down of Monarchs

The monarchs are leaving us
graceful royalty from beyond the mind's imagination
born from the deep Earth
with wingtips dipped in gold from the stars

They remind us with their presence
that we are more than mere bodies:
we too, must be from the stars
we who share the Earth with these creatures
are connected by the filaments of light
that shimmer through their
bright mosaic wings

The artists of the great cathedral windows,
those stained glass miracles reflecting sunlight,
must have felt their heartbeats flutter
in seeing those wings
creating fractals of geometric light
as the sun's rays bounced and played
on dancing colors
moving with the monarch's flight

The cathedrals remain
but the monarchs are leaving this Earth
their bodies dropping away
in numbers too large to fathom
in the span of time it takes
for a child to go from pre-teen to adult
or a field mouse to live its whole life
or a dream to die in a young child's mind

Astonishing the brevity of this rapid decline
after they have lived millennia on this planet
and we are the caretakers of their habitat
in this brief moment of extinction

On the coastline of California
where they have gathered year by year
their numbers now dwindle
from over ten million
to a mere two thousand
a slight flicker of what they once were

By the time you read this poem
more will have died
unable to spread their wings
and remind us of our own soul's light

They are following the way of
the Indian cheetah
and the Chinese paddlefish
the Yangtze River dolphin
and the Carolina parakeet
and more species of
bird and animal and insect
than we want
to count

I see them now
the monarchs
slowly moving their wingspans
in gentle flutters
as they perch on rocks and branches

giving us, perhaps,
the last fleeting glimpse
of heaven in this form
before the last one dies
its wings and body
returning to the soil

What weight we carry
knowing we may be the last
to see their gentle bodies in flight

They foretell our own destiny
our own exodus into flight

I grieve now
for what my grandchildren may never know:
> to share the Earth with these messengers of grace
> to feel the catch of wonder
> the stopping of the breath
> in the moment one lands on a nearby branch
> opening and closing its wings slowly
> then soaring
>   into a bright blue sky

MSW

Missing Otters

The coastal otter
seen as nothing
but a pelt
was shot
in the head

the fur trader
didn't care
that this otter
was a mama
who had anchored
her pup
into safety
by wrapping
her
in seaweed

the fur trader
didn't think about
seven generations

and that kelp beds
would diminish
because the population of
sea urchins
                exploded

Scientists delivered
twenty nine scared
otters from Alaska
but the skull and tooth size
and shape
were incompatible--
                they did not
                survive

The kelp bed stipes
are strong
yet flexible
so they can sway
to the rhythm
of ocean currents

They are trying
their best
to stay strong
to stay
in the face of warmer
temperatures
debris
and missing otters

ARA

15

Be Like Water

Be like water
that moves hard rock
to crumble

Move slowly through ravines
paved with pebbles
baking in the harsh sun

Wash over the dry and brittle
sagebrush, coaxing life back
to the springtime desert

Be like water
that does not give up
but must flow endlessly to the sea

Water that quenches
the burning thirst for justice
and the harsh burn of hatred

Water that is as old as the stars
and as new as this day's rain
washing the world alive again

Be like water
when hope is dying
and those around you cry out

Be the water
that does not preach
and does not back down

The water that carries pain to the ocean
and purifies what has become hardened
by grief we believe will never end

The Earth turns without asking permission
the wind blows without regret
the bird flies to carry the seed to its birth

Be like water in this time
of chaos and fire and
a world that cries for justice

The water will never dry up
on its journey home to the sea
and we, we must learn to swim in these tides

No matter how things swirl and turn now
be the water, breaking rock, soothing and healing
unrelenting

MSW

Connecting

Invitation

I am thinking now of the teeth of horses
the way a horse can seem to almost smile at you
mouth open, revealing what is usually hidden

The sharing of teeth is an intimate moment
when you can see what is inside:
that which is protected by the flap and curl of lips

A horse's teeth might be checked to see
if it is healthy, strong, worthy -
a benchmark of its usefulness

But now I'm thinking of the way a horse might
open its mouth wide and use those teeth
to bite into a crisp, red apple
the juice splattering from the force
of that powerful jaw

Something bold and beautiful arises
in that image:
teeth crunching down
broken flesh of the apple
the crisp sound of the crunch
the wet spray of the apple juice
the smile of the human standing nearby
the one who offered the apple
the one who loves the horse
the one who hopes for this moment of intimacy
in the fresh morning dew
when the horse will bare its teeth

reaching for that bite of apple
whinnying, tossing its wild mane in a moment of joy
bowing its head in a gesture of love

back to this human standing nearby
who is hoping for an invitation
to learn to be vulnerable
like this horse –
        wild, crunching, loving -
        baring all in this perfect moment
        of the first light
        of a new day

MSW

The Gift

I saw something
last night--
a shadow
on the rocks
that replaced
the bark
we now know
speeds up fires,
but I didn't
pay it
any mind
for fear
it was
a young skunk
separated
from its mother

This morning
I see with clarity
a blue-gray mouse
tranquil and beautiful
in its eternal sleeping—
a gift
for me
from the neighbor's cat
for letting it lounge
unperturbed
and free from the dog
her owner
has replaced
her with

ARA

Silent Flight

(to Ellen)

Sipping chai
with you
on this
late winter Sunday
as the winds of March
are already beginning
to blow toward us
such a simple, quiet moment
of pleasure

I am brought home
to moments of my childhood
I think of the flight
of birds in the marshes
the way they start low
to the water
barely skimming the brackish surface
with their bodies
then lifting slowly
bodies full of grace
they are silent
in their ascent

You could almost miss
the way the light flickers
from the water
if you take your gaze
from the quiet sight
before you too soon

So simple yet
so full of grace
so easy to miss
the miracle before you
when you forget
how fleeting each moment is
how delicate
are the wings that fly
and the way the light
falls on you now

MSW

Ocean Song

You began at your ankles
toes digging into the sand as the ocean pull
swirled a hollow beneath your feet

Stepping hesitantly at first
you moved into the waves
washing white onto the shore
after gently rolling past your legs

Suddenly knee deep
you turned to look at us
watching you from the shore
and we could only see the shape
of your face
guessing you wore a smile
before you turned back
to face the larger waves
crashing just beyond you

Slowly, step by step,
you moved deeper into the water
though you knew it would be cold
even icy
on your hips and waist

The pelicans dipped and soared above you
and in the distance I saw
a ship
or a whale
I do not know which
and the sun splashed light
brilliant
all around us

breaking into prisms
as it rolled with the waves
crashing ashore

I saw myself in you
just then
remembering waters
half a continent away
much warmer than these
waters that called and pulled
and beckoned me
to walk and wade
and swim deeper
into the sea
until everyone I loved on the shore
was only a distant dot
and the borders of my own body
dissolved into salt water
swirling sand
liquid light

When I finally swam back to shore
exhausted, exhilarated
I felt blinded by the splash of light
around everyone I saw

Sun-soaked, I dropped onto the beach
laughing

I see you now
daughter of my heart
pulled slowly, certainly
by the siren call of the sea

We watch you turn your face
up to the sun
salt water washing over you
a distant dot before us
pulled deeper with each wave

I am blinded
by the diamond light
swirling over you now
lighting you up
          like a living gem
                    of the brilliant sea

MSW

27

With Mom in the Sacred Garden on Kaua'i

Mammalove
vision: in the sacred grove
of trees from India
bright blue balls
at our feet
like magic candy
Mamma
wide-eyed
like me
crucifix on her neck
Ganesh, elephant
of joy
covered in leis
and me
barefoot
all of us smiling
light cascading through trees
connected
universal
love
Mamma

MSW

Similarities

A family
of grown people
despite differing viewpoints
discover
they are all
donors
and fearlessly talk
about death

and fearlessly talk
about life
that comes
from the twinning
of a liver
lungs
or kidneys
from the giving
of bone
cartilage
corneas
a heart--its valves and vessels
from intestines
a pancreas--
life void of politics
and full of second chances

ARA

Family Tree

Be a tree
with roots deep in the Earth
nurtured by the earthworms and
microbes nudging the Earth alive
in each moment
rooted by strength
roots connecting out
beneath the surface

Here, twined with the roots of
a sister tree
here, merging with the roots of
a tall pine
just below the surface
you are connected endlessly
in a web of strength
you know nothing about
a web of community
that wraps around the world

Here, linking with an oak tree
and, here
held safely by the Mother tree
the oldest tree of all

She smiles upon you
nudging you forward
nurturing you with her own
sap and sweetness

She is older than human memory
and you are an offshoot
of her very
Life Force

Stand strong
your life goes deeper
than you think

Let the world enjoy
your green leaves and vibrant flowers

Be a home for birds
and small creatures

Breathe deep into your roots
tendrils reaching far into the world
which loves you into being
each day

MSW

Healing

Redemption

Perhaps it is enough
    to share a cup of tea
    when winds of the world
    have blown us past
    what we think
    we can endure

To reach out and embrace
    a stranger or a friend
    whose child is terminally ill
    or whose mother
    no longer speaks coherently
    or even recognizes her child

Perhaps it is enough
    to read the news
    one story after another
    of democracy crumbling
    or bigotry taking root
    growing tendrils in hidden, fertile cracks

To pause after reading
    and say a prayer
    or write a forceful letter
    or stand in the street with a sign
    or link arms with the grandmothers
    who would die for their beliefs
    if they thought it would bring justice

I pray it is enough
    to write this simple poem
    light this simple candle
    hold my life up as a prayer
    a testament to the simple act
    of believing
            in everything I love
            in the redemption that must surely come
            from the bravery that it is
            to love this broken world

MSW

A Perfect Window View

cypress trees
the ocean
a mother in braids
and a hoodie
her boy
on the sand
flopping
like a seal

ARA

Restoration

the cold morning
has kept people
in their warm homes
nestled in flannel sheets
while we go
to the dirt path
with filaments of frost
that crunch
under our rubber soles

a brilliant sun
makes the elderberries
seem
like they're in
technicolor

two does
cross our path
unafraid:
a welcome

the creek
that had run so low
last summer
is almost
restored

the heady scent
of pine
of various kinds
is inhaled deeply--

all this
lets us forget
the virus
running rampant
out there

ARA

Manoomin

A COVID diagnosis
luckily mild:
a runny nose
some congestion
some time in quarantine
but our friend knows
that deep down
the diagnosis stokes
a small fear
in him
due to the loss
of his father
not even a year ago—to the same virus
so our friend falls
into what she does
so well

a chicken soup
which at first
may seem ordinary
for the usual suspects:
fine sliced celery
carrots
and chopped onions
but in it
is a magical ingredient
that conjures
in her Oregon kitchen
cold Minnesota nights
and the isolation
from friends
from the outside
made alright

by board games
and this warming soup
with wild rice
Zizania palustris
or what has been called
since time immemorial
Manoomin
which she stirs
on her stovetop
Manoomin
beloved by the red-winged blackbirds
and the waterfowl
seeking it
for nesting cover
in those Great Lakes.

ARA

Remembering

Travelling on the 101
an homage
to the everymen
of our lives
Cal Trans worker
Michael "Flea" Feliciano
and on a small stretch
further down
Braceros

I feel grateful
that finally
someone acknowledges
the way
Mexican men
saved an industry
while American men
went to war
men like Tio Alfonso
and Abuelito Rafael

Today
new everymen
and women
in hoodies
dot
the kale
artichoke
and strawberry fields
even during lockdowns
or days that suffocate

will anyone remember
them?
ARA

Girlhood Dreams

A stop
with trepidation
for burgers
our friend
recommends
in country
claimed by Trump

A surprise

A young woman
with rose
and La Raza
tattoos
in the Old English lettering
I recognize

Her partner
a man
with a shaved head
and a gold crucifix
displayed
against a starched
and impeccable
white t-shirt

remnants
of a world
I once inhabited
on the periphery

as we wait
for our food
standard oldies
in the background

remind me
of Gonzalo
Martha
and Nadine
remind me
of girlhood dreams

of being
switchblade tough
firme

and beautiful

ARA

Becoming the Woman I Am

The woman in the mirror
stares at me silently
I am just getting to know her
though she has been gazing at me
for many months
her eyes always asking:
Do I see her?
Will I claim her?

She has been patient with me
knowing I do not yet recognize
the small lines on her face
as my own
do not yet claim
the skin that sags a bit
below the jaw
or the way her eyelids fold
over eyes – still bright –
still waiting
for my final acceptance
of their changing shape and tone

She asks little of me
and I know she has
all the time in the world

It is only I who feel
the relentless rush of time
washing days and months and years
into faded memory

She, I know,
is wise enough to understand
that time, changing creature
that it is,
moves and paces itself
to its own rhythm
that it is not fixed
as I once believed
She lives in that deeper time
not counted in minutes
or hours
that moves like water
sometimes swiftly
sometimes barely stirring at all

The woman in the mirror
smiles silently now
gazing at me
beckoning

Come home, she whispers
come home

MSW

Twirling Through Space

Last night before sleep came
heavy and welcome
I drifted through scenes
of how things may end:
children leaving home
one by one
to find new worlds to call home
and the two of us
left behind
to find our way
in this home
we have made together
now empty of child-like laughter
and the singsong rhythm
of our daily lives

Before I drifted to sleep
my body tightened into fear:
how will I survive
as my body grows old
unto eventual death
with all the years of sunshine
stretching endlessly
behind me

Today it came to me
in a flash of light
or awakening
a gift from some
far off universe

or future I know
nothing about
calling me toward
whatever is beyond
this life and aging body

As sunlight dipped and glistened
through clouds above mountain peaks
on my drive home
suddenly I was there
spinning through dark matter
on a cart of steel
circling a track in spirals
Space Mountain
"Come, Mom, let's do this!"
they said
and though I was afraid
I joined them
"Sit with me and hold my hand"
I said, laughing, and
laughing, they did

Twirling through
that dark space
the wind whipped through me
and I squeezed their hands
laughing louder, and yelled,
"I love this ride!"

And I heard their sounds of joy
over the grate of steel
spinning over tracks of metal
rumbling and whirring
through dark space

We spiraled
with stars spinning by
and I held my breath

Maybe it will be like that
I thought today
as the sun lit through
my car window
as I drove down the highway
in this valley
we call home

Maybe it will be like that
I thought
and I heard us laughing
into space

We were laughing
all the way home

MSW

Good Send Off

A suit
is not selected

Instead
a pearl-button shirt
western pants
a black Tejana

Ramon Ayala
is singing
in the background

ARA

Guardian

Protect the sacred self
who lives inside
the one who came before
your tender body took shape

Protect the sacred self
from the relentless pull of doing
of drawer handles that must be repaired
and pots that must be washed
from the calendar beckoning
with your next appointment
and the tasks that run through your churning mind
waiting to be checked off
      they are never satiated
      and you are servant
      to their merciless
      never-ending call

Give your sacred self
a home, protected and fortified
from the hungry world

Draw a circle around it
wild with honeysuckle and roses in bloom
to keep out the ticking clock
and draw in the fresh scent of birth

Guard this shrine with your life
and return to it when the storms come in
and you cannot feel your breath
moving into your torso

Let this breath be your guide:
place your hand on your belly
and if it does not move from the
push of your gentle intake of air
if the breath stops
at your tightened chest

return to the home you have created
        trimmed with nature
        and protected by your holy vow:

To care for yourself
to return to yourself
to feel your spirit breath
moving deep into your limbs
        stilling your mind and body
        and the world's noisy clatter
        into the silence
                resounding without end

MSW

Ti'lomikh Falls

Afternoon healing
at the edge
of the Rogue River
where the white waters
carried
Olympic athletes
the only people
capable
in our time
to transport
a Takelma elder
in her quest
to reinstate
the Salmon
Ceremony

The contemplation
of earth-toned
river rocks
rounded by time
momentarily broken
by calls
from waterfowl
emerging
from willows

On the trail
back to the car
manzanita
Steller's jays

and the lingering smell
of what had been
a prodigious
berry season

Out of the corner
of my eye, a fishtail
            concentric circles

ARA

About the Authors

Alma Rosa Alvarez is a professor of English at Southern Oregon University where she primarily teaches U.S. Ethnic Literature. She is the co-author of *Promised Fruit* with Michelle St. Romain Wilson. She has a B.A. in English and Mexican-American Studies from California State University, Dominguez Hills and an M.A. and Ph.D. in English from University of California, Santa Barbara. Her favorite poets are Lucille Clifton and Gwendolyn Brooks, but she also has a special place in her heart for Pablo Neruda's odes.

Michelle St. Romain Wilson received a fellowship in 2022 for the Bookgardan women's writing program and will be a writer-in-residence at Craigardan in the Adirondacks in the fall of 2023. Co-author of *Promised Fruit* with Alma Rosa Alvarez, she is currently completing her first novel. She has taught English and creative writing to youth and teens in California, Hawai'i, and Oregon. She holds a B.A. in English from Loyola University, New Orleans and an M.A. in English/ Creative Writing from California State University, Sacramento.